A taste of....

CORI

C000182549

Recipes

Recipes

Text by Stuart Adlington. First published in 2011.
This edition published in 2011 by Myriad Books.
© Myriad Books Ltd 2011
PRINTED IN CHINA

Publishers Disclaimer
Whilst every effort has been made to ensure that the information contained is correct, the publisher cannot be held responsible for any errors and or omissions. Please note certain recipes may contain nuts or nut oil. The photographs in this book are for illustrative purposes only and do not represent the finished recipe. Photographs © Getty Images and Shutterstock.

A taste of....

Family holidays in Cornwall conjure up the most wonderful childhood memories - long, hot summer days sitting on the harbour wall in the beautiful picturesque fishing village of Mevagissy. Held tightly in one hand, a fluorescent orange fishing line disappearing into the blue waters below in the anticipation that a local brown crab may fancy taking a bite, and in the other hand a sugar cone topped with, the softest, creamiest, sweetest, ice cream I had ever tasted in my life, rapidly melting through my fingers.

Over the years, it appears very little has changed, still my favourite holiday destination in the British Isles, however my tastes may have matured with age, but still a child at heart, who still can't resist the old favourites. Maybe the flavour choice of the ice creams are a little more exotic, such delights as mango, papaya or pistachio sit happily along side the raspberry and chocolate varieties, but the old guard still valiantly remains, never to be out muscled by this invasion of flavours from distant shores in faraway places, the taste of real dairy Cornish ice cream is a delight to behold and savour forever.

The traditional and iconic Cornish Pasty, the quintessential Cornish cream tea, soft, freshly baked warm scones dripping with home made strawberry jam and served with lashings of rich dairy clotted cream, heavenly just heavenly.

Like many other seaside holiday destinations around our isles, the smell and taste of freshly cooked fish and chips eaten from the papers of yesterdays news, sat by the harbour, in my mind is really something really quite special, the senses are enhanced by the ozone.

With mile upon mile of rugged, naturally beautiful coastline to offer, it comes as no surprise that Cornwall has such a wealth and diversity of seafood and shellfish quite literally on it's doorstep. A Mecca for seafood lovers everywhere from mackerel to megrim, brill to bass and herring to hake.

With it's rich history of prized dairy cattle it is not surprising that there are numerous dairies and artisan producers, creating some of the highest quality cheeses. Cornish Yarg with its distinctive layer of nettles and the delicious Cornish Blue cheese has recently been voted the best cheese in the world.

Rich cakes and pastries can often be found flavoured, infused and coloured with the heady aroma of saffron, dating back many years when foreign sailors traded saffron for tin, being extracted from hundreds of mines across the county. A tradition of which has long since died out but the use of saffron in a variety of sweet and savoury dishes still lives on and thrives today.

CORNISH NETTLE and SPINACH SOUP

Serves 4

A really delicious soup once used as a spring tonic, nettles are high in Vitamin C and Iron. Traditionally, cooked sausages would be added to make the soup more substantial but this is purely optional.

Ingredients

900g/2lb young nettle tips, washed
900g/2lb spinach
1 1/2 pints chicken or vegetable stock
50g/2oz plain flour
50g/2oz butter
cold cooked sausages, chopped, optional
2 tbsps soured cream

1. Blanch the nettle tips in boiling water, drain and refresh. Place the nettles in a large saucepan, cover with the hot stock and simmer for 20 minutes, add the spinach and simmer for a further 5 minutes. Meanwhile, mix together the flour and butter to create a smooth paste. Blend the soup in a food processor until smooth.

2. Return the soup to the saucepan, bring to the boil, then add the butter and flour paste a little at a time, whisking continuously until the soup thickens.

3. Season to taste with salt and freshly ground black pepper. If using, add the chopped sausages, simmer gently to warm through, then spoon into warmed serving bowls and add a swirl of soured cream and serve.

Cornish Yarg

Produced from a recipe which dates back to the 13th century, Cornish Yarg was first conceived and produced in its present form by a couple named Allan and Jenny Gray, on their farm near Bodmin Moor.

It's unusual name is not derived from the Cornish language but is simply their name spelt backwards. The unique and most identifying feature is the edible outer jacket of nettles it wears. Unique to Cornish Yarg, and originally intended to aid preserving and as a mould ripening method, the nettles also lend his cows milk cheese a very distinctive flavour.

The leaves are picked locally and frozen to remove the sting, then carefully brushed on by hand. Yarg is a moist cheese with a fresh taste combined with a subtle and gentle tang. It is a semi-hard cheese, deliciously creamy under the rind and slightly crumbly in the core.

The current producers of the cheese, Cornish based, Lynther Dairies have also developed a variation on the original recipe for Yarg, enveloping the cheese in the leaves of wild garlic imparting a mild garlic flavour to the cheese.

Try the recipe overleaf which is a delicious variation on the umble cheese on toast recipe. Cornish Yarg Cheese, flavoured with Tribute Bitter from the Brewery in St.Austell.

CORNISH YARG AND TRIBUTE BITTER RAREBIT
Serves 4

Ingredients
350g/12oz Cornish Yarg cheese, crumbled
100ml Tribute bitter
1 shallot, peeled, finely chopped
75ml milk
75g/3oz butter
75g/3oz plain flour
1 egg yolk
1 tsp English mustard
pinch of nutmeg
4 thick slices crusty white bread

1. Melt the butter in a saucepan, add the chopped shallot and fry for 1-2 minutes, then add the flour and stir to make a roux, gradually add the milk, stirring continuously over a medium heat until all the milk has been absorbed and the sauce is smooth.

2. Stir in most of the cheese until melted, remove from the heat, then add, the egg yolk, mustard, and the bitter and stir well to combine all the ingredients. Season to taste with salt, freshly ground black pepper and a pinch of nutmeg. Leave the mixture to cool and thicken slightly.

3. Lightly toast the crusty bread, spread the cheese mixture over the top of the bread, sprinkle with the remainder of the cheese and grill for 3-4 minutes until golden brown and bubbling and serve immediately.

AN FRIED MACKEREL with HERB BUTTER

erves 4

>eliciously fresh Cornish mackerel, pan fried with herb butter,
uch a simple recipe, but its so quick and easy.

ugredients	*For the herb butter*
mackerel fillets, skin on	110g/4oz butter
5g/1oz softened butter	2 tbsps chopped fresh parsley
live oil for frying	squeeze of lemon juice
5g/3oz plain flour	
seasoned with salt and black pepper)	

o serve
rusty bread
mon wedges

. For the herb butter, mix the freshly chopped parsley and
mon juice together with the butter until well combined. Place a
ying pan on a medium high heat and add a drizzle of olive oil.

. Dip the mackerel fillets in the seasoned flour, dusting of any
xcess. Spread the flesh side of each fillet with a little of the herb
utter and place the fillets, butter side down in the hot pan.

. Cook the fillets for 2 minutes on either side, turn the heat
own slightly if the pan is getting too hot. Place the mackerel
llets on warmed serving plates with some extra herb butter to
ielt over the top. Serve with a wedge of lemon to squeeze over
nd some crusty bread to mop up all the lovely herb juices.

BAKED CRABS with CHILLI HERB BUTTER
Serves 4

Baked Crabs oozing with rich garlic and herb butter, the perfect
dish to eat with friends, finger food doesn't get better than this.

Ingredients
4 x 250-300g/9-11oz cornish brown crabs
175g/6oz butter
4 garlic cloves, lightly crushed, skin left on
1 red chilli, de-seeded, finely chopped
zest and juice of 1 lemon
2 tbsps chopped fresh parsley, retain the stalks
2 tbsps chopped fresh tarragon, retain the stalks
2 tbsps chopped fresh chives
splash of white wine vinegar

1. Preheat the oven to 180c/350f/Gas Mark 4. Blanch the crabs
in boiling salted water for 4-5minutes, remove from the pan
and set aside to cool slightly.

2. Melt the butter in a large ovenproof dish over a medium high
heat, add the herb stalks and garlic. Place the crabs in the
flavoured butter and cook for a few minutes. Turn the crabs over
in the butter until thoroughly coated, then add the lemon zest and
juice, chilli, and vinegar and place in the oven.

3. Bake the crabs for 8-10 minutes, basting the crabs regularly
with the herb butter. Remove the crabs from the pan reserving
the butter, then lightly crack the claws with the back of a heavy
knife.

. Place the crabs on a warmed serving platter, then add the chopped fresh herbs to the hot butter, mix well, then pour all the beautiful herb and garlic infused butter over the baked crabs and serve with a crisp green salad and lots of crusty bread to soak up all the butter. Simply delicious.

HOG'S PUDDING, SEARED SCALLOPS AND CIDER CREAM SAUCE
Serves 4

Spiced Hog's Pudding sausages, sweet succulent scallops, caramelised apples, served with a creamy cider and mustard sauce. The perfect combination, a wonderful dish for a hearty supper.

Ingredients
2 Hog's Pudding sausages, skins removed, cut into slices
12 large scallops
2 apples, peeled, cored, cut into wedges
olive oil
knob of butter
100ml cornish dry cider
50ml double cream
 tsp wholegrain mustard

. Add a dash of olive oil and a knob of butter to a large frying pan over a medium high heat until the butter is foaming. Add the hog's pudding and apple wedges and fry for 2-3 minutes until the apples and hog's pudding are lightly caramelised.

2. Push the apples and hog's pudding to the side of the pan, then add the scallops and fry for one minute on one side, then flip the scallops over, season with a little salt and freshly ground black pepper and cook for a further minute until they are golden brown but still soft and juicy on the inside.

3. Remove the scallops, apples and pudding from the pan and se aside and keep warm. Add the cider to the pan and simmer for 1-2 minutes until slightly reduced, add the cream and simmer for another minute, stir in the mustard.

4. Arrange the scallops, apples and hog's pudding onto warmed serving plates and serve immediately with the creamy cider sauce poured over the top.

CRAB SOUP
Serves 2-3

Hearty and filling but totally delicious.

Ingredients
225g/8oz crab meat, separate the white and dark meat
900ml/1 1/2 pints full fat milk, warmed
1.2ltr/2 pints hot chicken stock
50g/2oz plain flour
50g/2oz butter
2 tbsps dry sherry
pinch of grated nutmeg
150ml/1/4 pint double cream

1. Melt the butter in a saucepan, stir in the flour to make a roux, stirring continually add the milk, then the stock.

2. Add the dark crab meat and season with salt and freshly ground black pepper and simmer very gently for about 10 minutes.

3. Add the white crab meat and the sherry, continue to simmer gently for a few minutes to warm the crab meat through but do not boil, stir in the cream and serve spooned into warmed serving bowls.

OYSTER and PARMESAN GRATIN
Serves 2

Baked native rock oysters with a garlic and parmesan crust, for those who just can face the thought of eating them raw.

Ingredients

12 fresh oysters, shucked, shells reserved
50g/2oz butter
1 garlic clove, peeled and crushed
50g/2oz fresh white breadcrumbs
2 tbsps freshly grated parmesan cheese
1 tbsp chopped fresh parsley

1. Preheat the grill, then in a pan melt the butter and add the garlic and breadcrumbs and fry for a few minutes over a medium heat until the mixture is lightly golden and slightly crumbly. Remove from the heat, stir in the chopped parsley.

2. Place the oysters in their shells on a baking sheet, season with a twist of black pepper and top each oyster with the breadcrumb mixture and sprinkle over the grated cheese.

3. Place under the grill and cook for 4-5 minutes until bubbling and golden brown. Remove from the grill and serve immediately.

GRILLED CORNISH HERRINGS WITH A BUTTER, CIDER AND CHIVE SAUCE

Serves 4

Deliciously simple supper dish.

Ingredients
8 x herring fillets
olive oil
50ml/2 fl oz cider vinegar
175g/6oz chilled butter, cut into chunks
1 tbsp finely chopped chives

1. Preheat the grill to the highest setting. Place the herring fillets skin side up on a lightly oiled baking tray, season with salt and freshly ground black pepper and drizzle a little oil over the top.

2. Place under the preheated grill for 2-3 minutes until the skin is crisp and golden brown.

3. As the herrings are grilling, bring the vinegar up to boil in a small pan, then gradually but vigorously whisk in the butter a few pieces at a time until you have a smooth sauce. Stir in the chopped chives and season with salt and freshly ground black pepper if required.

4. Place the herrings on a warmed serving dish and spoon the hot butter sauce over the top.

MUSSELS IN A CORNISH CREAM, SAFFRON AND WHITE WINE SAUCE

Serves 2-3

Mussels cooked in a cream, saffron and herb infused sauce. Simply beautiful served with lots of fresh crusty bread to soak up all the lovely juices.

Ingredients
1.5kg/3lb 5oz fresh mussels, washed and cleaned, discard any that don't close when tapped.
pinch of fresh saffron strands
50g/2oz shallots, peeled and chopped
50g/2oz butter
100ml/31/2fl oz double cream

MUSSELS IN A CORNISH CREAM SAUCE/CONTINUED

200ml/7fl oz white wine
1 bay leaf
1 sprig fresh thyme
1 spring fresh tarragon
chopped fresh parsley to serve
200ml/7fl oz fish stock

1. In a large pan, melt the butter, add the chopped shallots and fry gently for 2-3 minutes until tender but not coloured. Add the saffron, bay leaf, thyme, tarragon and white wine and bring to the boil.

2. Reduce the mixture by half, then add the cream and fish stock and return to the boil. Add the mussels to the pan and place a tight fitting lid on the pan, then give the pan a good shake.

3. Once the mixture has returned to the boil and the mussels have opened, strain the mussels in a colander over a pan to collect the sauce. Discard any mussels that have not opened.

4. Gently heat the sauce until it has reduced further, season to taste with salt if required and plenty of freshly ground black pepper.

5. Place the mussels into a large serving bowl and pour the cream sauce over the top. Sprinkle with freshly chopped parsley and serve immediately.

STARGAZY PIE

Serves 4

A traditional fish pie recipe from the small fishing village of Mousehole, the unique feature of the dish are the fish heads protruding through the pastry crust gazing at the stars above.

Ingredients

pilchards, herring or small mackerel, filleted, residual bones removed, heads and tails reserved
25g/1oz butter
25g/1oz flour
onion, peeled and finely chopped
tbsps white wine
250ml fish stock
00ml double cream
tbsps chopped fresh parsley
hard boiled eggs, shelled and sliced
200g/7oz puff pastry
egg, beaten

. Preheat the oven to 200c/400f/Gas Mark 6. Melt the butter in pan and gently cook the onions until soft, stir in the flour and mix well.

. Gradually add the fish stock and wine stirring continuously to create a smooth sauce. Simmer gently for 5 minutes then add the cream and simmer for a further minute or two.

. Stir in the sliced egg and chopped parsley, season well and remove from the heat and set aside.

4. Cut the fish fillets in half and lay them into the base of a shallow pie dish and season with salt and freshly ground black pepper, then pour the sauce over the fish.

5 Roll out the pastry on a lightly floured surface to a thickness of about 3mm. Lay the pastry over the dish and trim the edges. With the excess pastry, roll out again, then cut out small star shapes, these will be used to decorate the top of the pie.

6. Cut small incisions in the pastry and push the reserved heads and tails through the pastry so they are protruding out. Place the star shapes in the gaps between the fish heads and tails and brush the pastry with the beaten egg.

7. Bake in the preheated oven for 40-45 minutes or until the pastry is well risen and golden brown and the sauce piping hot and bubbling. Remove from the oven and serve.

Tin Mine Ruins, near St. Agnes

Lizard Peninsula

Polperr

CORNISH GAME HENS WITH ROSEMARY, LEMON AND GARLIC

Serves 4

Rock Cornish Game Hens make the most perfect single serving, simply roasted with rosemary, garlic and lemons, so simple so delicious.

Ingredients

  Cornish game hens
  lemon, cut into quarters
  sprigs fresh rosemary
 live oil
 2 garlic cloves
 plash of white wine
 75ml/10floz chicken stock

. Preheat the oven to 200c/400f/Gas Mark 6. Place the Cornish ens in a large roasted tray, then season the inside with salt and reshly ground black pepper. Divide the rosemary, lemon and arlic cloves and place inside the hens.

. Rub the hens with a good drizzle of olive oil and season well. our over the white wine and chicken stock and roast in the oven or 50 minutes or until the birds are golden brown and the juices un clear from the legs when a skewer is inserted.

. Remove the birds from the oven, scrape out the rosemary, emon and garlic from the inside of the birds and add to the oasting pan. Cover the birds with a sheet of tin foil and set side to rest.

4. Place the roasting tray over a medium high heat and boil rapidly to reduce the sauce, making sure you scrape all the lovely sticky bits of the bottom of the tray with a wooden spoon.

5. The garlic will be beautifully sweet and tender, use the back of the wooden spoon to squash the garlic into the sauce.

6. Discard the lemon and rosemary, then, pour the sauce over the top of the hens and serve with delicious buttered Cornish new potatoes and steamed seasonal vegetables.

THE TRADITIONAL CORNISH PASTY

The Cornish pasty undoubtedly, the most famous and iconic of all the foods from the region. The pasty originally evolved to meet the needs of the tin miners. A hearty and substantial meal wrapped in a pastry casing made it a very practical lunch in the dark, damp and dirty condition the miners had to endure.

Tradition has it that the original pasties contained meat and vegetables in one end and jam or fruit in the other end, in order to give the miners a two course meal. There is still much debate as to whether the crimp should be placed on the top or on the side, however one thing is certain, is that the crimped edge was used as a handle to hold the pasty, eaten with the miners dirty hands, the crimped edge was then discarded.

There are, however, some facts that can be agreed upon, the meat should always be chopped, the vegetables finely sliced and the ingredients must never be cooked before they are wrapped in the pastry. Each pasty must be baked completely from raw. It is this fact that makes the Cornish Pasty unique amongst similar foods from around the world.

CORNISH PASTIES
Serves 4-6

Ingredients for the pastry
450g/1lb plain flour, plus extra for dusting
2 tsps baking powder
1 tsp salt
125g/4 1/2 oz unsalted butter
2 egg yolks
125ml/4 1/2 fl oz cold water

Ingredients for the filling
300g/11oz beef skirt or braising steak, finely chopped
1 tbsp plain flour
150g/5oz onion, peeled, finely sliced
150g/5oz swede, peeled,finely sliced
450g/1lb potato, peeled finely sliced
50g/2oz butter
salt and freshly ground black pepper
1 egg, beaten for glazing

1. Begin by making the pastry, sieve the flour, baking and salt into a large mixing bowl, rub in the butter using your finger tips until the mixture resembles fine breadcrumbs.

. Add the eggs yolks and a little of the water until the mixture omes together to form a dough. You may not need all the water, o add a little at a time.

. Wrap the pastry in clingfilm and chill in the fridge for half an our.

. Place the chopped beef into a bowl, then add the flour and nix until the meat is well coated. Season with salt and lots of reshly ground black pepper. Add the thinly sliced vegetables to he meat and mix to combine all the ingredients.

. Preheat the oven to 180c/350f/Gas Mark 4. Remove the astry from the fridge, then roll out on a lightly floured surface.

. Using a large plate as a template, cut out the pastry into discs. Divide the filling onto the pastry rounds, making sure there is a ap around the edges of the pastry.

. Brush the pastry edges with the beaten egg,then carefully ring the pastry up from the sides and over the top to encase the illing. Using your fingertips crimp and twist the top of the pastry o create a twisted plaited edge.

. Brush the pasties with the beaten egg, place on a lightly reased baking sheet and bake in the preheated oven for 45 ninutes, or until the pastry is beautifully golden brown and the illing is piping hot. Remove from the oven, leave to rest for 10 ninutes then serve.

CORNISH CRAB, LEEK AND SAFFRON PASTIES
Makes 6

Delicately flavoured Cornish crab meat, soft buttered leeks
infused with saffron make these pasties such a treat.

Ingredients
900g/2lb puff pastry
1/2 tsp saffron strands
2 tbsps hot water
350g/12oz white crab meat
75g/3oz brown crab meat
225g/9oz leeks, trimmed, thinly sliced
50g/2oz fresh white breadcrumbs
1 tsp salt
freshly ground black pepper
25g/1oz butter,melted
1 egg, beaten for glazing

1. Preheat the oven to200c/400f/Gas Mark 6. Roll out the pastry
on a lightly floured surface and cut into six 19cm/7inch circles.

2. For the filling, soak the saffron strands in the hot water for 5
minutes. Place the white and brown crab meat, sliced leeks,
breadcrumbs, salt and pepper into a bowl, carefully stir together
until well combined.

3. Add the saffron and water together with the melted butter into
the crab, leek and breadcrumb filling and stir carefully to
combine all the ingredients.

. Divide the filling between the pastry discs. Brush the edges of
he pastry with the beaten egg, bring both sides of the pastry
)gether at the top and crimp to seal the pastry together.

. Place the pasties on a lightly greased baking sheet, brush the
asties with the beaten egg, then bake in the preheated oven for
5 minutes until golden brown and crisp. Remove from the oven,
eave to cool slightly then serve. Delicious eaten hot or cold.

CORNISH BRILL WITH STEAMED CLAMS
erves 2

'an fried brill with sweet steamed juicy clams infused with
arlic and wine make this simple recipe such a beautiful dish.

ngredients
 brill fillets, skin removed
 10g/4oz clams
 0ml white wine
 00ml fish or chicken stock
 sprig of thyme
 clove garlic, peeled, finely chopped
 shallot, peeled, finely chopped
 live oil
 uice of half a lemon
 sick of celery, finely chopped
 eshly chopped parsley

. Heat a drizzle of olive oil in a pan, add the shallot, celery,
arlic and fresh thyme and fry gently for 2-3 minutes until
ie onions are tender.

2. Add the white wine and simmer for 5minutes or until the win has reduced by half. Add the stock and bring to the boil, reduce the heat, then simmer for a further 5 minutes until the stock has reduced slightly.

3. Heat a frying pan until hot, add a drizzle of olive oil and fry the brill fillets, for 2-3 minutes on either side until lightly golden brown. Remove the fish from the pan and set aside to rest and keep warm.

4. Meanwhile, pour the clams into the stock, place a tight fitting lid on top, shake the pan well and cook the clams for 2-3 minute or until the clams have opened. Discard any that remain shut. Sti in the chopped fresh parsley and divide the clams and broth between two warmed serving bowls. To serve, place the brill fillets on top the clams and serve immediately.

CORNISH BLUE CHEESE SALAD with PEARS
Serves 6

A beautifully simple salad packed full of flavour, delicious as a starter, light lunch or supper dish. Voted the best Cheese in the world in 2010, beating 2600 entries from 26 countries around the globe to win this prestigious title, Cornish Blue is a vegetarian cows milk cheese, dry salted by hand before being left to mature for between 12-14 weeks. The blue veins are made by piercing the cheeses each week with metal rods, allowing them to air, thu helping the blue mould spread throughout.

Cornish Blue is designed to be eaten as a young cheese, the flavour is beautifully mellow and sweet with a soft creamy texture.

Ingredients

225g/8oz crumbled cornish blue cheese
ripe pears, peeled cored and sliced
large bunch of watercress
large bunch of rocket leaves
0g/20oz walnuts, halved

For the dressing

tbsp balsamic vinegar
tbsps olive oil
freshly ground black pepper

. To make the dressing, simply combine all the ingredients and mix well to combine. Place the watercress and rocket in a large serving dish, scatter over the sliced pears and crumbled blue cheese.

. Pour over the dressing, then carefully, using your hands toss the ingredients together until all the ingredients are coated in the dressing. Scatter over the walnuts and serve.

35

CORNISH CREAM TEA
Serves 8

Delicious warm scones, home made strawberry jam and fresh clotted Cornish cream served with a refreshing pot of tea, the perfect British afternoon treat.

Ingredients
225g/8oz self raising flour
pinch of salt
1 tsp baking powder
50g/2oz butter
25g/1oz caster sugar
150ml milk/1/4 pint milk
1 egg, beaten for glazing

. Preheat the oven to 220c/425f/Gas Mark 7. Sift together the flour, salt and baking powder into a large bowl. Stir in the sugar, add the butter and using your fingertips rub into the flour to create a fine breadcrumb consistency. Add the milk a little at a time to form a smooth dough.

. Roll out the dough on a lightly floured surface to a thickness of 2cm/3/4 inches. Using a 5cm/2inch cutter, cut out the dough, using one sharp downward cut, do not twist the cutter as this will result in an uneven rise during baking.

. Brush the top the scones with the beaten egg, ensuring no egg wash drips down the side of the scone as this will hinder the rising. Leave the scones to rest for 15 minutes.

. Bake in the preheated oven for 10-12 minutes until golden brown. Remove from the oven, allow to cool slightly and serve while still warm. Serve lightly buttered with strawberry jam and generous spoonful of clotted Cornish cream on top.

STRAWBERRY JAM
Yields approx 3kg/6.6lb

Ingredients
kg/4 1/2 lb strawberries
Juice of 3 lemons
kg/4 1/2 jam sugar
Small knob of butter

. Place the whole strawberries in a large non metallic bowl, add the sugar and lemon juice, gently stir together, then cover with a tea towel and leave to stand overnight.

2. Place a saucer in the freezer. This will be used to test the jam has set to the correct consistency later. Tip the fruit and juice into a large preserving pan or a 4.5 litre/8 pint heavy based saucepan. Heat gently, stirring to dissolve the sugar, do not boil until the sugar has dissolved.

3. Turn up the heat and boil hard for 4 minutes, take off the heat and test for setting point. Spoon a little jam onto the cold saucer. After a couple of minutes gently push your finger through the cold jam, if it wrinkles up the jam is ready, if not re boil for a further 2 minutes or until setting point is reached.

4. Take off the heat and swirl in the butter, if the scum doesn't dissolve skim with a slotted spoon. Leave to cool for 10 minutes.

5. Stir gently to distribute the fruit then pour into warmed sterilised jars, top with a cellophane disc and seal with a tight fitting lid.

Store in a cool dark place.

SAFFRON CAKE
Makes 1 loaf

A traditional Cornish cake, the addition of the saffron gives the fruit loaf a beautifully deep yellow colour and heady fragrant aroma.

The use of saffron has been used for centuries, it is said to be have introduced to the the region by Phoenician sailors landing on the ruggish Cornish coast to barter with saffron in exchange for tin.

Ingredients
500g/lb 2oz white bread flour
1 tsp salt
a good pinch of saffron strands
150g/5oz unsalted butter, diced
50g/2oz light muscovado sugar
7g sachet of dried yeast
300ml/10 fl oz hot milk
110g/4oz dried mixed fruit, currants, sultanas, raisins

39

1. Place the saffron strands in the hot milk, give it a really good stir and leave to infuse. Lightly grease a 2lb loaf tin with butter.

2. Place the flour and salt in a large mixing bowl, then using your fingertips rub the butter into the flour until the mixture resembles fine breadcrumbs.

3. Add the dried yeast to the mixture and stir well to combine al the ingredients. Reheat the saffron infused milk until tepid, then mix the warmed milk into the flour.

4. Using your hands work the liquid into the flour to form a dough. Turn out the dough onto a lightly floured surface and knead well for about 10 minutes. Add the dried fruit into the dough and mix well.

5. Place the dough into the greased loaf tin, cover lightly with clingfilm or a large plastic bag. Leave the dough to double in size in a warm place, this will take about an hour, or until the dough rises to the top of the tin.

6. As the dough is rising preheat the oven to 180c/350f/Gas Mark 4. Bake the loaf in the preheated oven for about 45 minute to an hour, or until the top of the loaf is beautifully golden browr and the base should sound hollow when tapped. Remove from the oven, allow to cool on a wire rack and cut into slices when cool.

CORNISH SCRUMPY CAKE

The perfect tea time treat.

Ingredients
5 tbsps Cornish cyder/scrumpy
225g/10oz dried mixed fruit, (sultanas, currants & raisins)
175g/6oz butter
175g/6oz light brown sugar
3 eggs, beaten
225g/8oz self raising flour
2 tsps mixed spice

1. Soak the dried fruit in the cyder for at least a couple of hours but it's best to leave overnight if you have the time. Preheat the oven to 180c/350f/Gas Mark 4.

2. Cream together the butter and sugar until pale, light and fluffy, gradually add the eggs one at a time, beating thoroughly between each addition.

3. Sieve the flour and mixed spice into the creamed egg and butter mixture Sir in the soaked dried fruit and stir well until thoroughly combined. Spoon the cake mixture into a greased and lined 22cm x 7cm deep loose bottomed cake tin.

4. Bake in the oven for 50-60 minutes or until well risen and golden brown and a skewer inserted into the centre comes out clean. Remove from the oven, leave to cool slightly in the tin, then remove from the tin and allow to cool on a wire cooling rack.When cool, cut into slices and serve with clotted cream.

CORNISH FAIRINGS

Delicious crisp ginger biscuits, the name Fairings is derived from the sweet biscuits that were traditionally sold at fairs and feasts.

Ingredients
110g/4oz plain flour
1 tsp baking powder
1 tsp bicarbonate of soda
1 tsp ground ginger
1/2 ground cinnamon
50g/2oz butter
50g/2oz caster sugar
4 tbsps golden syrup, warmed

1. Lightly grease 2 baking trays and preheat the oven to 200c/400f/Gas Mark 6. Sift the flour, baking powder, bicarbonate of soda and the ground spices into a large mixing bowl.

2. Rub in the butter until the mixture resembles fine breadcrumbs, stir in the sugar and warmed syrup to create a stiff dough.

3. Divide the dough into 20 pieces and form each one into a ball. Place the dough balls on the baking sheet spaced well apart and bake in the preheated oven for 8-10 minutes until the biscuits are golden brown.

4. Remove from the oven, allow the biscuits to cool on the tray for a few minutes, then transfer to a wire cooling rack to cool completely.

CORNISH SPLITS
Serves 8

Soft, sweet and delicious, split buns, filled with clotted cream and raspberry jam.

Ingredients	*To fill*
450g/1lb plain flour	raspberry jam
10g/1/4 oz dried yeast	clotted cream
25g/1oz butter, melted	
300ml warm milk	
3 tbsps caster sugar	

1. Preheat the oven to 200c/400f/Gas Mark 6. Sieve the flour into a large mixing bowl, add the yeast, melted butter and sugar and enough warm milk to create a soft dough. Remove from the bowl then knead the dough on a lightly floured surface for 5-10 minutes until smooth and elastic.

2. Return the dough to the bowl, cover with clingfilm and leave in a warm place until the dough has doubled in size. Divide the dough into 8 equal pieces and roll into small buns. Place the buns on a lightly greased baking sheet, cover loosely with oiled clingfilm and allow to rise and double in size once more.

3. Brush the buns lightly with milk and bake in the preheated oven for 10-12 minutes until well risen and very lightly golden brown. Remove from the oven and allow to cool. Using a sharp knife, cut the buns at a slight angle and fill with raspberry jam and a generous spoonful of rich clotted cream.

CLOTTED CREAM RICE PUDDING AND FRESH RASPBERRY SAUCE

Serves 4

Rich, creamy & totally indulgent, Comfort food at it's best

Ingredients
110g/4oz clotted cream
570ml/20fl oz full fat milk
500ml/18fl oz double cream
50g/2oz butter
200g/7oz pudding rice
1 vanilla pod, split, seeds scraped out

For the raspberries
50g/2oz caster sugar
300g/10oz fresh raspberries

1. In a large saucepan, add the rice, vanilla pod and seeds, milk, sugar and cream and slowly bring to the boil stirring regularly. Once the mixture has boiled, reduce to heat to a very gentle simmer, cover with a lid slightly ajar stirring regularly to avoid the rice catching on the base of the pan.

2. Cook for about 30-40 minutes until the rice is perfectly soft and plump and the rice has absorbed the majority of the liquid.

3. Meanwhile as the rice is cooking, Place the raspberries and sugar in a small pan over a high heat and cook for 2-3 minutes until the sugar has melted and the raspberries are soft. Remove from the heat and set aside to cool slightly.

4. When ready to serve, stir the clotted cream into the rice pudding and heat through. Spoon into warmed serving bowls and top with a generous spoonful of the warm raspberry sauce.